THE DARK SIDE OF THE EARTH

ALSO BY PAUL ZWEIG

Against Emptiness
The Adventurer
The Heresy of Self-Love
Lautréamont: The Violent Narcissus
Selected Poems of Yvon Goll (Editor)

HARPER & ROW, PUBLISHERS
New York, Evanston, San Francisco, London

THE
DARK SIDE
OF THE
EARTH

Paul Zweig

Grateful acknowledgment is made to the following magazines in which some of the poems first appeared:

The Nation: "We Have No Dead," "The Encounter," "The Dark Side of the Earth."

The American Poetry Review: "To a Thin Man," "The Lover," "Robinson Crusoe's Notebooks," "Listening to Bells," "Answering the Storm" (under the title "Sentences").

Poetry: "The Black Stone," "The Failure of Narcissus."

Iowa Review: "Liberation Manual."

The Columbia Forum (New Series): "Laughing for Your Life."

Partisan Review: "The Archeology."

The following poems appear with the permission of the magazines in which they first appeared:

Sumac: "Three Deadly Voices," "A Song," "Keeping the Peace," "Meditations on My Skeleton."

Seizure Magazine: "The Face of Not Talking."

Twelve Poems/Skywriting: "Saying New Words," "To the Red Angel," "The City of Changes."

The poems "After the Creation," "The Hospital," and "Uptown" © 1973 *The New Yorker*.

FIRST EDITION

Designed by C. Linda Dingler

Library of Congress Cataloging in Publication Data

Zweig, Paul.
  The dark side of the earth.

  Poems.
  I. Title.
PS3576.W4D3   811'. 5'4   73–14302
ISBN 0–06–014817–9

To my mother and father

CONTENTS

PART ONE

PART ONE

GETTING OLDER

Advancing into sleepless woods,
Each year the ice getting thinner,
And the trapped waters darker;
The mind's frosty ballet superbly staged
On a floor of nerves;
Breath shorter, skin veined and rough;
Understanding a woman's precarious beauty
For the first time,
I stand in a frozen year,
And hear the whisper of darkened lives.
Do the words come from inside or out?
That sort of knowledge eludes me now.

Sometimes, when I go for a walk,
I see an old man's face smiling without humor.
His fleshy lips resemble an ear
Moving cautiously without any sound.
He waits for me at the end of a milky street
Which turns unpredictably into swamp or rust.
It is the old man I may never reach,
Distracted by everything that must be lived,
My hands twitching like butterflies in the brief sunlight.

THE HOSPITAL

I

When you see me driving
Through traffic,
Speeding, putting on the brakes,
You think:
"He knows what he is doing,
Where he goes
Everything is settled."

But the nights on Rikers Island
Are filled with dwarfish faces.
They sit up with me on sleepless nights,
Bargaining with insomnia.
They tell me that I am broken,
Mended by silence.

II

You hang over me in the white gloom
Like a pear
That will not ripen.

You are my hospital, I ask you for a pencil.
I say: "I want to write you a letter."

Your eyes are shells scrubbed by waves,
White sea-prints through which I see
The wards of predictable terror.

Sometimes the doctor comes in
And takes my pulse.

III
I believe the hospital walls,
My illness
Which only a stone could diagnose.
And I know, quivering doctor,
I know the eyes awake in the stuttering heart;
The bunched muscles of horses climbing the air,
Wild horses, not ridden or seen,
But the dying man sees them.
He cries out for rescue.

THE DARK SIDE OF THE EARTH

December 1972

We don't talk about the war anymore,
Living on the dark side of the earth,
The winter side,
Yet we do not keep silent either.
We repeat ourselves until the words
Become thin as insect husks,
Forgetting the stripped faces, the soup of limbs
Left when bombs have fallen.
It is dark here, a peculiar winter.
The ice storm caught us unawares
And we froze into busy postures and went on living,
But the inmost room in our bodies was a grave.
How else could bombers inch across the sunlight,
And the earth get drunk with shudders,
And the dead be indistinguishable from mud,
If our most comfortable nightmares
And our innocent wealth did not belong to death.
When words make nothing happen they turn against the sayer.
We are eaten by our words, and so are silent,
And don't talk about the war anymore.

UPTOWN

A streak of car paint;
A shopping cart dragged past the window
By a closed black face.
The worst is when the sidewalk becomes a mirror,
And the woman becomes a mirror,
With her abstract smile, her teeth like thrush eggs.

Thin child-body in November, why do you
Pass by me? Lovely freckled girl,
Naked inside those wraps of clothing,
Or maybe not. Maybe you are dressed
Underneath too, like an old armchair,
A crucifix of gray patched cloth,
But no bare touches where the secrets grow,
Soft as mushrooms underneath.

A boy hanging behind the bus wants to fly.
He squats on the rear fender, wondering
What that spread-eagled shape is grinning at him
From the scarred pavement, like Michelangelo's Prisoner.
Broken arms, yellow grin. No wings, but rising
From the mirror with the flexible haste
Of internal injuries.

In the middle of Broadway a tree strips down for winter.
It reminds me of Robinson Crusoe
Who sat on his island, winter and summer,
Moving his lips with squirrely haste,
While cars and buses grunted by him on both sides.

He too stripped down for winter long ago.
Now, alone among the carnivores,
Face creased like a prune, he is master
Of all he surveys, and blind to boot.

The sky darkens. Old men hurry home before the knives.
It is odd to think our movements come from within,
As if gusts of wind blew from each separate bone;
Each of us a hurricane—calm eyes, violent flesh—
Making memories for windless days.

ANSWERING THE STORM

My words are not sung, they are not spoken.
They crowd under my skin,
They die and are buried in the graves
Of my skin.

I see the unread poems in store windows:
A fire hydrant with two black nipples,
Men kissing in a doorway with lips like razor blades.
An alarm gallops in the street
Spreading quiet among the deaf who listen,
Thinking they hear.

The mourners cannot keep still,
Their laughter shakes in the grass.

You can answer the storm only with a storm,
The quiet only with a deeper quiet.

Sunset pours in my fingers.
Despair is a room where teeth flash
But not words,
Lips but not hungers.
You turn over on the bed,
Waves hiss onto the rocks;

Near the beach, a white seal wallows
In pale water.

I answer you, running from the half-opened mouth
Which brays behind me.
Are those prayers it cries?
I don't think so. Wounds, yes.

THE LOVER

A stone crushes you when you breathe.
You feel weary,
Like freezing in a snowdrift.

What kind of life kills itself anyway?
What are its tools?
A few drinks, a little talk.

You lean against the window
Knowing you could jump
If you wanted to.

Your feet echo
As you go downstairs,
Walking stiffly against the wind.

You don't stop to buy a newspaper,
You wait absently for the green light,
Smiling at the doorman of the cold house

Where your lover waits,
His beak gagged open, his wedge-shaped tongue
Trembling.

THE WAY DOWN AND OUT

When darkness flows in every movement I make,
A mirror with no face in it but mine,
Wide lips, thin bones,
A face built from secrets,
I go down through tunnels of cold earth,
My eyes heavy,
My stomach gathered to a knot.

—The blossoms lie dead but waiting,
Crushed but gathering strength.

I find comfort in the rock with my pursuers!
Naked, without smiles,
No handouts to the mutilated faces
Of the blacks.
Only quiet rippling in water
Like lovers' hands undressing in darkness,
Or the hush of an Egyptian grave
Preserving bread disdained by the gods,
Kept sweet in the mouth of darkness
By Thoth, who sleeps under each grain of corn,
Singing to the earth,
Singing to the brown girls in spring
Who moisten the black soil, whispering:
"Thoth moves in my belly,
Thoth rubs his thighs in my belly."

Thoth, god of black stems,
And children whose anguish laps against the flesh,

God of screams,
God of hot flowers scouring the intestines,
God of sweet candy,
And the sleep that comes without fail.

LOSING A FRIEND

When the anger finally came
We were startled to find how much we already knew
About dead friendships,
Breaking the words off, shoving the ends
Into each other's faces.
During those long walks along the Drive
We argued about men whose guts were clothed in talk,
Not knowing we were talking about ourselves.

Had warfare always existed in your muscular face?
Had my anger spurted for years
From deeps I never knew,
Silted over in the furthest bottom of myself?

I can smell the charred earth, windows
Gaping like broken mouths,
And the killing that goes on because a man
Keeps to what he knows best. Meeting on the street,
We will nod and say a few words, or pass and say nothing.
Yet we remain strangely intact in each other's minds
Like bodies buried yards deep in stone,
Without warmth or change,
Until our shadows stretch thin as drums,
And the time wearies of itself.

THREE DEADLY VOICES

I

THE WITNESS

He comes back from the quiet world
Stripped of words and explanations.
Aroused by a mute body, he kills and sleeps,
Sleeps and kills, saying
With each twist of his hands, here are words,
Listen!

II

THE KILLER

To kill, strangling stones until they dream
The forms we see,
Like a ring of Druidic slabs
Ripped from their sockets in the earth,
The wounds lovely with grass.
These boulders hurt the backs of men
Crazed with their dignity,
Longing to be the dark stones they carried.

III

THE VICTIM

My shape is an accident,
I contain the mystery of no-shape.
I am the victim clumsily offered, who outlives
His conquerer. I am stupidity, duration.

To murder I respond with gratitude:
A cloister of secret shapes emerging to express me.

One day I will call them back to me,
Wiser to have died, to have continued as earth.
I record each act like a day in my endlessness.
To kill is to age me with the beauty
Of these hazardous shapes, so frail I cry
To feel their doom, like a change of weather,
A veil of wind across my grassy oceans.

THE ARCHAEOLOGY

I

My first God was a tenement:
Warty red bricks, a net of cast iron
Slanting down a wall.
It looms in the before-dawn sweat,
Offered through the window as a covenant
That we survive each night;
That days float out of the stale darkness,
Busy with miracles.

II

We are married to each other's nights;
The sky a gray slice over a brush of trees.
It is Parmenides' world, the temptation of stone,
Where all lives are the same.
A dog whimpering is a heart, a butcher's rack is a hug,
A blind man is a mirror, a pistol is a gulp of blue wine.

III

My anxious lies will be discovered by archaeologists
In the tenth layer, under burnt ships
And the broken bones of horses.
They will have the apologetic look of hearthstones,
Singed by the ordinary sadness of living.

That was before the virus of heroes had ruined our minds.
I grew up with no biography
As stones grow up, or the weather.
It was like fishing without a hook.

In the city of the tenth layer
The son had not ripped fire from his father's loins,
Wisdom was not a virgin born out of an ear,
The soldier did not stink from secret wounds,
The poet had not invented silence,
His wife had not yet learned to love death.

When the diggers came, they found burnt pots,
But the shadows had fled.
Instead of songs, a coprolith;
Instead of heaven, scratch marks on a wall,
The relic of bad dreams.

IV

I want to gnaw at my jailer's shadow.
I want to write to my brothers in crime
Whose victims get rich,
While they squat in stale rooms
Rolling snake-eyes with their heart-bones.
I want to sing of claustrophobia,
The iron marriage of a man to his shadow.

Hugging the sprawled sheets, the grease,
And the insomnia;
Inspecting the entrails of birds;
Speaking ghost-talk to my wife
Although my anxiety shines through her
Without casting a shadow;

I will praise the fear of death
Which is the basalt of dark foundations;
I will trace a map for caravans setting out
Tomorrow across the blinding floor.
I will tell my secrets, listening in secret
To find them out.

V

I did not write these words; I scraped them into stone
Like a prisoner loosening the bars with his bare hands.
My poem is an empty window, and a leap to freedom:
Softly blinking leaves, the horizon
Cupped suddenly under the sky.
It is a long fall as birds do it,
Shorter this way.

PART TWO

PART TWO

AFTER THE CREATION

I

Beetle dozing in the moist clay,
Your bright shell
Pumping like a heart;

I watched you crawl
In the striped darkness of the shed,
Resembling an eyelid drooped in the dirt,
A wilted prayer
Smelling of pepper and dead books.

Rust clenched into brightness.

II

From you I inherit my patience
With pure horror;
My faceted eyes, all but one of their gleams
Turned inward;
My self-knowledge; my dread of footsteps.

Because your scrapes and clicks
Are brothers to the small tongues of earth.
Because in my solitude you outnumber me;
Because, like God, you are everywhere;
Because the world is manna to beetles.

III

I dreamt my heart was a beetle.

23

It brushed my skin with bare wires,
And I had the revelation of stone.
It twitched in the passageways of my throat.
It ate me from within, creating hunger
And the seasons of flesh;
It died and left me with a book of skin,
My only honesty.

IV

But when the beetle unfolds its stubby wings,
When its eyes wander like watery pins,
There will be nothing.

No childhood killed over again
Before your eyes.
Nothing to crawl through the insomniac streets,
Adrift in the ominous peacefulness
Of work and love.

The chitinous claw descends like a snowflake,
And the beetle of the first day,
The life-lode,
Starts over again its countdown toward nightmare.

AMANITA PHALLOIDUS

To be alone in the woods, poking at the moist odors
For mushrooms, knowing the diffuse sexuality
Which comes after a long rain has soaked the forest floor,
And the sun has begun its languorous tattoo
Past the chestnut leaves, and the dark pointed branches.

Around me lie the dusky skins of mushrooms.
I love these shade-gnomes
Meditating in the brown whisper of leaves.
They spring up and melt away in days,
Leaving behind a meaty smell which the wind dissolves.
After each rain they glide back again, standing idly
In the mottled quiet, like Homer's ghosts
Staring at travelers in the underworld.

Here is one I recognize.
I get down on my knees, and scrape away
The furry twigs around its base,
Its green head shaking imperceptibly.
Amanita phalloidus:
Sexual head poking from the moist loam at my feet.
In these gnarled woods, the old confusions return.
The earth's erection is a mother phallus,
A pale eye nodding in the temple of my knees.
Leaning over, I see its speckled skin,
Its fish-white spores,
Its milky egg sifted over with soil.

I know that one bite would be suicide,
Like a pause in the wind, when the fainter hum
Of insects can be heard. I am not tempted,
Yet I find it hard to look away,
As if I were kneeling over a well
Whose moist echoes urged me to lean over more,
Still more, until my arms lurched forward,
And I fell into the perfect night of the earth.

ROBINSON CRUSOE'S NOTEBOOKS

When I am alone,
The world becomes an erotic dream.
Sex boils in my shoes,
I plunge my penis into every open flower.
Bushes sway, pendulous and ripe;
I touch them timidly.
On my hilltop of erect green leaves
The other words are gone:
Friends, lovers, acquaintances;
The quiet surrounds them like a moist palm.

My skin explores the earth.
Pine shadows touch me, and I yield,
Wading in their milky darkness,
Afraid to have a name,
Afraid it will search me out
Like a shirt of weariness.

Silence is sex,
Solitude is sex.
The unused body blossoms into sex.
Earth color of marmalade,
Failed wells inside me spitting dust
And broken stones,
Suddenly you are filled with water,
Like a hand kneading my soft flesh,
Drooped over me by the slow wind of sex,
And the warm wind of sex.

I remember the smile of a woman
Who hadn't spoken for three days,
Her lips smelling of cold ash,
Her stomach flat as a wish;
A woman with no hungers.

Her hands were tunnels,
She had faces I had never seen.

Her face of cold grass,
Breasts whispering to themselves;
Her face without music
Bent inward like a prayer;
Her face of rain misting slowly, bitterly.

When she talked,
Loaves of quiet heaped
In the green light of the café.

Convalescing after a deep wound.
It is June, and they are cutting hay.
The obedient stalks fall silently all one way.
As the fields are put in order,
I too lie down all one way,
Obedient to the memory of pain,
Abiding by its wish.
Inside me, the ache of healing,
As if I prayed with my flesh.
Even the scar resembles a language
I must learn.

What is left when pain goes away?
Not a body, not even expectations.

The animal goes on twitching
After it is dead.

I have been broken,
As light is broken when it penetrates water;
As storms break,
And marriages splinter in a calm sea.
I have reached dead water.
I don't even frighten birds,
They settle on my hand.

All the loneliness in the world
Gathers here,
Billowing toward the sun.
It will rain, they say.
But rain is food,
And loneliness doesn't give,
It takes.

The scratching noise of a cicada,
Branches floating at different levels in the forest,
An ant lost on a sea of pink trousers.
Suddenly a deer browsing a few feet away,
Me frozen still, not blinking or breathing.
He must smell me, because he backs off
Cautiously between low-hanging branches.
Meat-eaters are lonely,
They smell of danger.

After several days of not talking,
The words leave you.
Every sound becomes their voice:
Pear tree, wild clover.

A pair of blue wings settles near my foot.
The stones resist my impulse
To explore their resistance to pain.
Even peace becomes warfare.
The insanities taste you, and it is good.
Will you consent to crawl among them,
Knowing your children?
Will you taste the brackish pond water,
Wallowing in grass,
Your face covered with green scum?

You pick your way through high grass
Like a bird confused by headlights.
You are the image staring up out of the pond,
And the space the branches close behind.
You take the shape the wind takes
When it enters a room.
You have learned the charity of taking;
A circle that cannot close, and yet is perfect.

LISTENING TO BELLS

I hear bells ringing in the village,
Filling the valley with their deep liquid sound.
They mean that someone has died today,
Maybe the old woman on the hilltop facing mine.
She dressed in black for so many years,
Death was paid for on arrival; it came like the lover
She took half a century ago, when vineyards
Grew where the woods are whispering with bells.

Sometimes I've tried to visit the church
On a ruined back street of the town.
It's always locked, except for pigeons nesting
Under the eaves, and for the dead
Who have the key. They pull the bell rope
Hanging down beside the altar,
Pumping the sound of death out into sunlight.

Bells ring over the oaks and the walnuts;
Over this house cast away in grass, acacia thorns,
And those dark thorns turned inward
Like a dream of terror.

The valley hums with the news death flings
Over its woods and fields, over its heaps
Of damp stone left by the Druids,
Remembered now only by wasps and spiders,
But touched, almost trembling, by the bells
Rolling past, even when the church
Has been locked again, and strands of rope

Touch the floor in one moist heap,
And there is no sound I can hear
Except my life whispering, bell-like,
In the patient morning.

A SONG

I looked at the earth until the earth looked into me,
And the smell of chestnut blossoms made me sleepy;
And the forest, like a rotten quilt, warmed me and chilled me.

A chestnut trunk shivered beside me
As rain hit the leaves and rolled free.
My lives stood up in speckled sunlight and talked with me.

Their voices were muffled by wrecked leaves and moss.
A breeze crept in their faces, their words were lost,
Like a handful of seeds dropped on the yellow moss.

THE FAILURE OF NARCISSUS

I

A pool of water
Scooped in the flat of a rock.
When I look into it I see nothing,
Not even my face;
Only a trap door of ripples.

Dizziness grabs me under my shirt.
It's a long way into the red weave of trees,
A long chilly way.
The black wingtips of a hawk
Lean against the wind.

II

A chalky quiet seeps under trees
And rubs against the white stone cliffs.
My face opens wide, exposing a face of uncut stone.
Painstakingly I write down these words,
Trying to reach you from the face where I am shipwrecked,
Inhuman, recalling the movement of lips
Like waves along a beach.

KEEPING THE PEACE

I would like to write for nobody.
To hide my words under a stone
And wait for an answer, questioning
The roar of branches in the night wind.
Is it for me? Is this the criticism
I can expect?

THE FACE OF NOT TALKING

Wind whose secrets are told
In the chestnut wood;
Butterfly toppling toward me, flower-high;
I hang on to you, needing your help
Against the creatures of silence,
Smooth wanderers made of not talking,
Of stumbling day by day
Into the face of quietness.

THE ENCOUNTER

Come close and hug me, strange faces,
Flesh-makers,
Treading down the grass beside me
In the world, where I am alone
To be with you, delicate-toothed,
Slack-jawed mothers.

SAYING NEW WORDS

I

After wind scooping at the woodwork
Like a knife blade,
And my hands leaving their skin behind them
On the smooth edge of sanity;
After forty nights like forty thieves,
And forty days like forty doves
With no news,
I stand outside and it is spring.

II

Warm spring night that cannot fool me;
Walnut branches reluctant to give up
Your winter wisdom, which is death, not calm;
Fish-shaped cloud, your underbelly
Blind with sunlight, although I prefer
The part of you that is in mourning;
Grapevine buried alive, without leaves or flowers;
I spared you once, now you are getting ready
To outlive me.

III

But now I want to say new words to you:
Grass whispering
In the straw-bodies of old sentences;
The hush of flowers on a bare branch;
Birds gnawing holes in the silence;
Stones like guilty children, reluctant
To speak at all.

PART THREE

PART THREE

MEDITATIONS ON MY SKELETON

I

When you're in the tomb, use the language of the tomb. When you're talking to yourself, turn the words until they face you.

One advantage of being in the tomb is that you don't have to lie, because the truth doesn't matter either.

What do you take with you into the tomb? The energy of life, but all its aims are left outside. The energy without its aims is what your death is made of.

From it has been removed the wrapping, everything particular, everything that bears a name. They're gone.

II

When you're in the tomb, you're anxious for everything to be recorded. You want a record, you want it to be well written.

You want your parents to admire it, despite the pain it causes them to face so much truth all at once, even if, in fact, you're lying.

Now that nothing can possibly happen, you want every word to be completely accurate. So you write, if you can, about some-one else who is in a different tomb.

III

Let me describe to you my grave clothes. I am wearing clean underwear, tight corduroy pants, a blue and red striped shirt.

All clean, fitting me well. My appearance is beyond reproach.

When spoken to, I say the answer contained in the question. I think I am loved, but that is the sort of thing I can no longer say I know.

IV

Air moves freely around my bones. I am concerned about the grass and flowers, to which my ancient fat has been so useful.

It is good to have been useful. And now a breeze of melancholy stirs in my tomb, as my grass-flower being takes its natural course, and my use comes to an end.

V

My death is being celebrated. Unlike true dead men, I have not been invited. For the moment I am a subject of conversation, famous in my way. He died, they say, not knowing what else to say.

Why don't you discuss my qualities? How he was selfish but devoted to his parents. Unyielding, but full of charm. Make up some things. How his poetry was read by all, and found to be the ultimate word on simple things. How some people even believed what he wrote, although he didn't.

But I did believe it when I was alive. Some of my dreams—dead men do dream—still believe it. To believe anything at all causes a stone to be sealed in place. Dead men avoid that.

TO THE RED ANGEL

Isidore Ducasse, Count of Lautréamont

I

A man reveals himself to a tree
Along Riverside Drive.

Light falls from his narrow face
And his incomplete eyes;

While the sperm of lonely men
Lie jewel-like on the leaves.

II

Dawn of blue milk and rolled newspapers;
Dawn of incantations, when the poet
Spits into a dried well,
And water the color of arsenic spurts forth;

Your moth-eaten black cloak,
Your face like the wing-span of a bat,
Are impatient.

The lamp-carrying vampire has slept too long.
The crabs in the caves of the flesh
Are anxious and pale.

III

The stick woman stands in a glass booth
With her mouth tilted open,
Giving a piece of her mind to the stale air:

"I want you to know what's on my mind,
I want you to know about floating.
It's sleeping out, why don't you
Keep me warm? Are you listening,
Are you a victim?"

I know you, dark specialist,
Knife-point of trembles,
Telephone with your guts hanging out.

These are your streets
Where everything eats itself alive.

IV

Lautréamont, my vampire,
My exile,
I'd give a lot to know what you looked like,
Who your lovers were,
What desert baked in your skull
When you wrote out fables for the new Kabbala,
The book of cruelties.

You walked in the early light
Among dog turds, picnic wrappers
And the astonished green of city grass.

You said nothing, but your lips moved
And a bird leapt out;
From the jaws of the bird, a fish;

From the fish, a jackal with moonlike teeth.
From the open wound crawled a quiver
Of scales and saliva.
It was your birthright, and you clung sucking
To its belly.

V

You possess the key to a room without windows.
Around the table a crowd eats and drinks
Without sound. There are boys and mothers,
Pale ladies in green velvet, lace cuffs.

Sometimes the room trembles. You wake up,
And peer through half-closed eyes
At the table where a new guest eats and drinks.
You see the scar at the base of his neck
Where you dreamed him.

VI

Once I found a stone angel.
Its wings were humped,
Its eyes halfway between murder
And pleading.

Maybe its chipped face
Was an image
Of the killer sharpening his tools
In the smiles of happy men.
Lautréamont, that angel is the face

I give you.
It is yours, for nothing.

VII

When you died, Paris was at war;
People starved in the streets;
The ghost inside you hugged by a deadlier ghost.
And this is what killed you:
The horror at no longer being alone.

WE HAVE NO DEAD

I think of an Indian who is not confused
By plumbing and thick pavement,
But walks to a bleak valley under the street
Where he lay on the raw earth one winter night,
Hungry, muscles aching with the effort to be still.
He received his name from that quiet valley,
First Winter Snow they called him. Now he descends
Between electric cables and the stifling odor of tar,
To where sumac pods rasp in the wind,
And leafless twigs spurt from the frozen slicks.

Earth mixed with child-dust,
Bee sounds, coughs of the wind:
They are sounds made by the dead
Who stroke our breasts and touch our mouths,
Making words out of great silences.
For only the streets of the city can be wholly empty.
Their grime-colored walls, the flat words of man-speech
Mutilate the dead as we are mutilated,
Knowing only daylight and throats of flesh
And trees without names.

You come in the colorless hours,
Piercing the invisible wall we build in our flesh
To divide us from the dead. We call it life,
Pitifully ignorant of what our cells know,
Rising from the undisturbed floor and the graves of seed,
Into our faces which move ponderously, masking
The heaven of the dead.

TO A THIN MAN

I

Thin man eating your way through death,
Famished old bones, thinning out your hunger
Along roads, where a yellow field lengthens into darkness.

You are the third person in my privacy,
Your face pieced together out of wounds,
Smiling now and then like an eclipse,
A scorched earth policy of smiles.

When I share myself out to silence
You mourn for me,
Pronouncing hunger to be the sacrament,
Starvation the prayer book,
But the mystery is lean bones.

II

Thin man, I am climbing your backbone,
Arms roughening into branches,
Legs groping in the earth like stepladders.
Below, the earth sucks in your tears.

Only nameless flowers grow there:
Odd-shaped beggars from another world,
Housed in the mad grass of the fields,
They are your children.

III

A crossroad stares under one thin light,
Like the arms of the sleeper crossed over his tomb.

Thin man, through your eyes I see the terror
Of beginnings and endings.
I hear bird cries fragrant as the old religions.
Only the sleeper's heart rumbles
In the combed teeth of the cottonwood trees.

INSOMNIA

I

Insomnia is the long way around.

I think of colorless faces, who choose
The assignation of sweat and smell and too much time.
They go where the sleepers go, but they do not hurry,
Sending each part of their body to a separate death.

II

You sit beside me on my red sofa,
It is like sitting alone.
Shadows from a passing bus crawl over the floor;
They remind me of men, lips caked with gray,
Walking limply from streetlight to streetlight.

III

But now even the poor are sleeping,
And the old people in their green rooms,
Faces almost innocent as they practice
The leap into death. I watch them
In torn black coats, athletic and solitary,
Lips chewing bits of memory, like old bread.

IV

We sleep fitfully,
Pinned to our beds by an enormous weight.
The night is soft, pulpy as a bruise.

We cover over this wound with our faces.
Our ambitions bandage it, our talk soothes it.
We are a way of forgetting the night.

LAUGHING FOR YOUR LIFE

The idea of the poem is humorous,
Like a heaven of whales,
Or a fortune told in insects' wings.

You can see it rolling toward you
On the crest of an earthquake
Until all you see reflected is an eye,
Some fat rubber bands rolling around,
Like lips.

Poetry does that to your face,
Heaving on its crest a skin of lies,
An ecstasy, something completely unexpected
With its pants down, and you start to laugh,
Forgetting your name and the word
For poetry, forgetting what it's like
To be drowned in your aging skin,
With the tide coming in.

THE BLACK STONE

I

Death was my first appetite,
I've had others since.

Black stone I swallowed on the day I was born,
You are the loneliness fattening in my breath;
You cross out each word I stumble toward,
Saying help.

On mornings of smooth stone,
And mornings of grass curled, pale and dreamy,
Underneath the stone,
I know you are a nugget of black ice
Working your way down inside me.

II

You are closer to me than flesh,
You are the knot of loose ends I breathe;
A tear wept
In the closed weather of the stone.

Sometimes when I'm bored or sleepy
I can feel you under my eyelids,
Incredibly patient;
You take a lifetime to go from here to there.

III

It is raining along the beaches.
Beads of slowness shining on tree trunks
And on the windshields of blind cars.

It is raining over the Atlantic,
Falling in the space between lips.

Black stone lifting against gravity,
The democracy of small moments has arrived.
Notes merge and thicken to a roar.

In the ocean of the dying, we are all fish.

LIBERATION MANUAL

I

When I landed on earth
I saw the moon-bones blood and flesh
Of the dumbest women in America.

The graves in my skin sprang open;
Instead of bones there were flowers.

Around me, heads burst into bloom.
It was the revolution I had been waiting for,
The true communism.

II

Exposed in a root like William Blake,
I met the recording angel.

"What have you got in that book of yours?"
I asked.

"I've got a man killing his face
Under the peaceful face he wears,
And the ceremony of hate performed by air.
I've got a man talking with the perfect pitch
Of the death instinct."

When I looked again, the recording angel
Had shrunk into a fist of pure screaming,
A heart-print of smoke.

III

I arrive in a valise packed with nails,
Talking with poets,
Strolling in their poems.

As far back as I can remember I am no fish,
In this life or the last.
My longing for freedom is a mystery to me.

Asleep on a light bulb,
I dream of personal dawns.

I am so private, I cast no shadow.
Grass does not bend where I walk.
The machinery of my smile is beautiful
As the footwork of the malarial fly
On still water,
Beautiful as the laughter of politicians.

IV

Armed with a mirror,
Opinions to hide my hunger,
I inhabit the stones of the road.

If I keep on going I will reach the end,
My skin falling off,
My bones individually laughing,

On vacation forever
In the long summer of death,
Like an aging clown,
Cured of personality.

THE SENTENCE

An eye stares at me
From the dark connection, as I head out of December
Into another ending.

Softly the body fails.

I am the victim in a room, composing letters
To myself.
It is the small talk prisoners know.

PART FOUR

THE CITY OF CHANGES

Venice 1973

I

Returning to thunder, white buildings,
And a damp smell rising from the sidewalk.
Lightning plunges through me, exposing
The gray wall I lean against
Like Rodin's half-carved statues.

I feel sympathy for the motionless water,
It is a mirror with no gift for images,
A cat's eye attuned to the miracle of loneliness,
Maneuvering in the shadowy space with sure feet.

Remembering too much or too little,
I have the solidity of a rainstorm,
Beating sudden fingers into oily water,
Molding myself minute by minute
To this beautiful grave.

II

What comes from water must return to it;
First the image goes, later we follow.

This passage over black sand,
This passage between names we know as thirst;
Searching for shadows where the light fails and we begin,
Bearing maps, compass, legible stars,
And a sound rising in concert that does not touch the silence,
Merging, cell by cell, into one bodily song.

Listen!
It is the city subsiding into patience
Under rose-colored bricks;
It is the green anguish of doorsills;
It is the tide feeling its way along marble steps;
It is a floor for echoes;
It is the impossibility of touching what we see,
Carried further by death, so much further.

III

These are the changes we know:
A desert whispering into flower,
A lover betrayed,
A tree choosing its darkness.

Each day we fail, sitting in forgotten chairs,
Changing our sex, our color,
Loving what we hate.
We choose our death over again.
Like a bride without smiles
We marry the stone husband who hugs us,
Our perfect shadow, inscribed with our name.

My exhausted eyes, my face
Staring up at me from the water,
Are traveler's wounds.
Beneath them hides the life the wild man saw
Like a sediment in his cup of visions.

IV

Adrift on the surface of death,
He caressed its images, and they spoke to him,
Stirred by a strange wind which crept out of roots,
Rasping and sighing, for they spoke with his own breath:

"Come into the marketplace,
Come into the city of changes
Where we live, as in a mirror.
Having given up your name, you will move
Across the space of death without hindrance.
You will be a link between all things,
A road of images.

"The heavy flesh of dahlias,
Their translucid green stems,
Whatever smolders in its own sunlight,
—Bird, fish or man—barters its name
And its memory in the marketplace of death.

"You will be the bridge and the water under it.
You will be the soil and the root.
You will be the blood and the vein it flows through.
You will be the rock and the wind.
The poem plunges in your flesh,
Its needle wounds you. You are its food.
Only in you can the poem become alive."

V

We are a soil for violent flowers.
We eat envy, anguish is our poem.
Yet things become beautiful in our company.

This day is cool and bright.
Behind each gate geraniums burst like glances,
The ocean extends its patient fingers between the buildings.
The peace we cannot live surrounds us,
Penetrating the pores of buildings.

It is our gift to another century,
Like the unburied ghosts of heroes
Who walk at night and leave their messages.
Things grow old in it and become human,
As we cannot do.